Sept. 29, 2016

Dear Emily,

Look for the cat on every page. Enjoy!

Best,
Isabelle Fonvig

A TRUE STORY

THREE WORLD TRADE CENTER WAS OUR HOME

BY ISABELLE TADMOURY FLORIJN

ILLUSTRATED BY
ANNEROSE WAHL

DEDICATED TO THE PEOPLE
WHO LOST THEIR LIVES
IN THE MARRIOTT
WORLD TRADE CENTER

"HI, MY NAME IS ISABELLE. I'LL NEVER FORGET MY NINTH BIRTHDAY."

MY FATHER WAS THE GENERAL MANAGER OF A HOTEL SQUEEZED BETWEEN THE WORLD TRADE CENTER TOWERS IN NEW YORK.

WE COULD SEE THE STATUE OF LIBERTY FROM OUR SUITE WHERE WE LIVED WITH OUR CAT, FELIX AND RABBIT SASHA.

"READY, SET, GO!" MY SISTER AND I LIKED TO CHASE FELIX DOWN THE LONG HALLWAY TO THE OTHER END OF THE BUILDING.

"SORRY, COMING THROUGH!" I YELLED AT THE BELLMAN.

"WATCH OUT!" MY SISTER YELLED AT THE LADY. FELIX WAS A FAST CAT.

"I'LL CALL SECURITY TO SEE IF THEY CAN HELP US FIND FELIX," MY MOM SAID. WE DECIDED TO MAKE SOME POSTERS AND HEAD DOWN TO THE LOBBY.

"FELIX, FELIX WHERE ARE YOU?" WE WERE WORRIED, THE HOTEL IS A BIG PLACE. MY SISTER WAS SO UPSET THAT MY MOTHER SUGGESTED WE GO ROLLER SKATING FOR A FEW MINUTES TO GET OUR MINDS OFF FELIX.

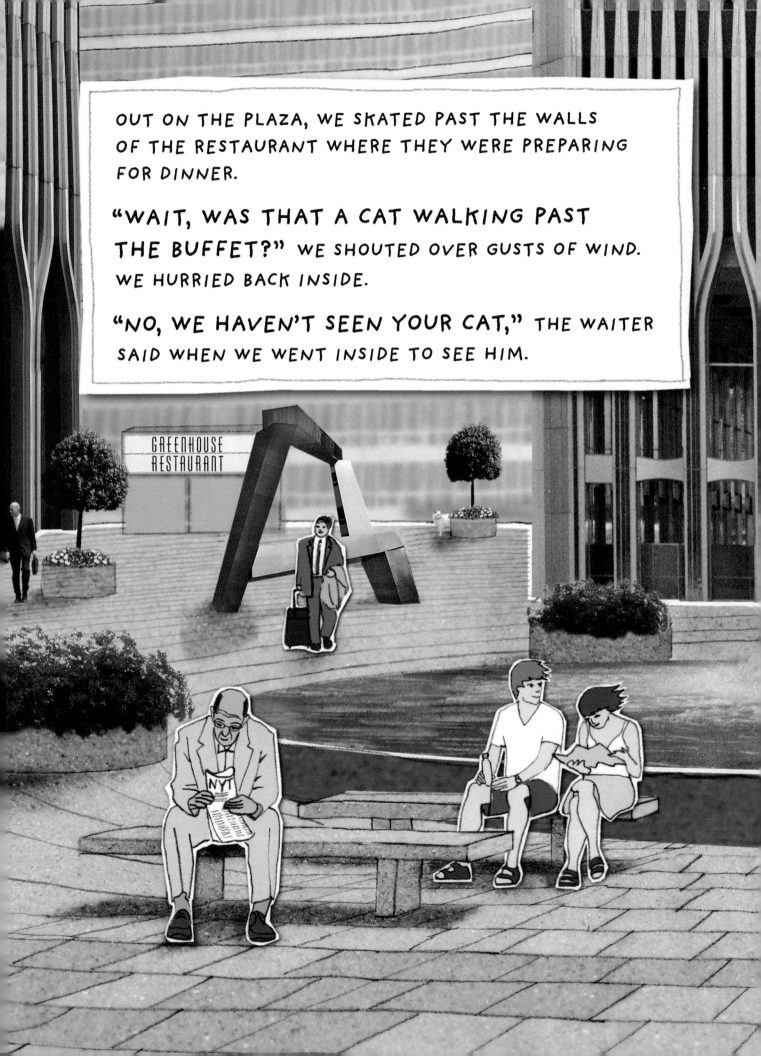

OUT ON THE PLAZA, WE SKATED PAST THE WALLS OF THE RESTAURANT WHERE THEY WERE PREPARING FOR DINNER.

"WAIT, WAS THAT A CAT WALKING PAST THE BUFFET?" WE SHOUTED OVER GUSTS OF WIND. WE HURRIED BACK INSIDE.

"NO, WE HAVEN'T SEEN YOUR CAT," THE WAITER SAID WHEN WE WENT INSIDE TO SEE HIM.

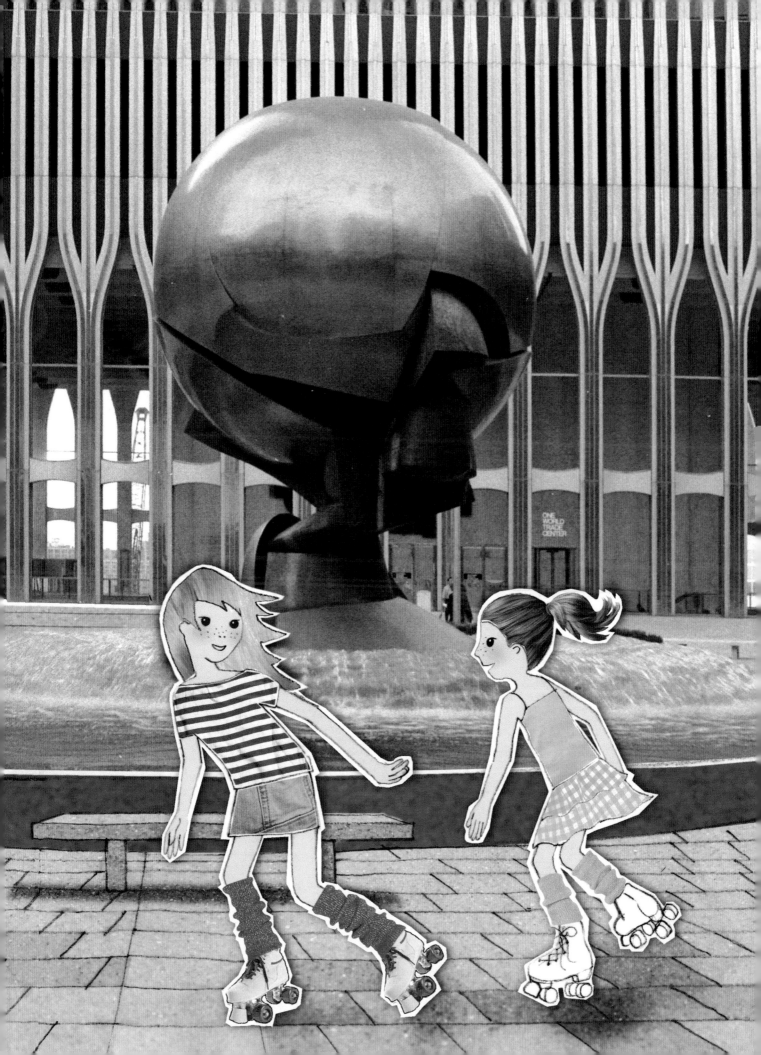

"IT'S TIME TO MEET YOUR FRIENDS AT THE WINDOWS OF THE WORLD RESTAURANT," MY DAD ANNOUNCED WHEN HE FOUND US. "I DON'T FEEL MUCH LIKE HAVING A BIRTHDAY PARTY IF WE HAVEN'T FOUND FELIX. CAN WE HANG UP SOME MORE POSTERS FIRST?" I ASKED HIM.

ON THE WAY TO THE NORTH TOWER, WE TAPED POSTERS ANYWHERE WE COULD FIND A SPACE. IN THE ELEVATOR, WE HAD TO SWALLOW HARD TO POP OUR EARS. 107 FLOORS IS A LONG WAY UP. I HOPED THAT FELIX HADN'T COME THIS FAR.

MISSING!
WHITE CAT "FELIX"

HAS GREEN EYES
LOVES CHOCOLATE CAKE
CONTACT: 212-632-9970

"WOW, LOOK AT THE VIEW," WE COULD
SEE ALL THE WAY FROM NEW JERSEY TO QUEENS.

"I PREFER THAT PART BEST," CARYN SAID
AS SHE POINTED TO THE EMPIRE STATE AND
CHRYSLER BUILDINGS.

WHEN ALL THE WAITERS CAME OVER TO SING "HAPPY BIRTHDAY" THEY DIDN'T SEEM TO NOTICE WHAT WE WERE NERVOUSLY WHISPERING ABOUT; THAT THE TOWER WAS MOVING EVER SO SLIGHTLY.

MY FATHER EXPLAINED THAT THE TOWERS WERE DESIGNED TO SWAY WITH THE WIND AND THAT THIS WAS NORMAL FOR THE WORLD'S TALLEST BUILDINGS.

AFTER LUNCH, WE ALL RAN BACK TO THE HOTEL TO LOOK FOR THE CAT. "I'LL GET HIS SQUEAKY TOY MOUSE" "AND I'LL BRING HIS FOOD BOWL, MAYBE HE'S HUNGRY" MY SISTER ADDED.

"FELIX, WHERE ARE YOU?" WE WERE GETTING TIRED. "MAYBE HE'LL SECRETLY FOLLOW US BACK TO OUR SUITE..."

THE DOORBELL RANG AS SOON AS WE GOT THERE. "I'M SORRY, WE HAVEN'T ORDERED ANYTHING SO I DON'T THINK THIS IS FOR US," SAID MY MOM TO THE WAITER. HE SMILED.

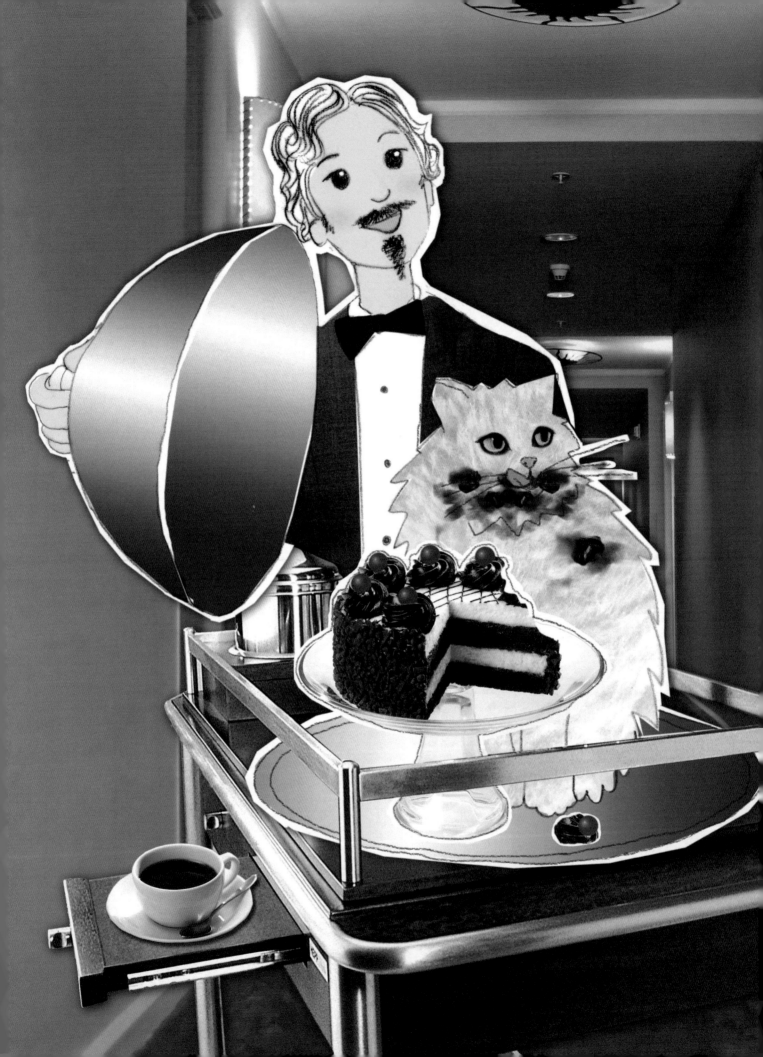

"LOOK WHAT I FOUND ON MY TRAY!" HE SAID AS HE LIFTED THE DOME. THERE WAS FELIX EATING A CHOCOLATE CAKE! HE HAPPILY JUMPED OFF THE TRAY BACK INTO THE APARTMENT. WE GAVE OUR CAT A BIG HUG. NOW WE WERE ALL COVERED IN CHOCOLATE CREAM.

TO MANY PEOPLE, THE WORLD
TRADE CENTER IS A TRAGIC PLACE.

FOR ME, IT WILL ALWAYS REMAIN
IN MY HEART AS MY HOME FILLED
WITH MANY HAPPY MEMORIES.

ADDITIONAL FACTS:

IN 1981, MY FATHER OPENED THE VISTA INTERNATIONAL HOTEL, OPERATED BY HILTON INTERNATIONAL. THIS WAS THE FIRST HOTEL IN DOWNTOWN NEW YORK SINCE 1839. IT WAS LATER TAKEN OVER BY MARRIOTT INTERNATIONAL.

THE 22-FLOOR AND 825-ROOM HOTEL WAS BUILT ON THE SAME FOUNDATION AS THE TWIN TOWERS SO MANY PEOPLE REGULARLY WALKED THROUGH THE BUILDING TO GET TO THEIR OFFICES.

ON SEPTEMBER 11, 2001, HUNDREDS OF PEOPLE FLEEING THE NORTH TOWER ARRIVED IN THE HOTEL, WHERE WORKERS STEERED THEM TO THE STREET EXIT FROM THE TALL SHIPS BAR.

WHILE THERE IS NO EXACT ACCOUNT OF HOW MANY CASUALTIES THERE WERE, WE DO KNOW THAT TWO HOTEL EMPLOYEES AND AT LEAST 40 FIREFIGHTERS, WHO WERE USING THE LOBBY AS A STAGING GROUND, PERISHED THAT DAY.

Made in the USA
Charleston, SC
29 August 2016